TODAY'S SUPERSTARS

Jonas Brothers

By Jayne Keedle

Gareth Stevens
Publishing

HUNTINGTON CITY TOWNSHIP
PUBLIC LIBRARY
255 WEST PARK DRIVE
HUNTINGTON, IN 46750

D1197724

Please visit our web site at www.garethstevens.com.
For a free catalog describing Gareth Stevens Publishing's list of high-quality books,
call 1-800-542-2595 (USA) or 1-800-387-3178 (Canada).
Gareth Stevens Publishing's fax: 1-877-542-2596

Library of Congress Cataloging-in-Publication Data
Keedle, Jayne.
    Jonas Brothers / by Jayne Keedle.
        p. cm. — (Today's superstars)
    Includes bibliographical references and index.
    ISBN-10: 1-4339-1970-2   ISBN-13: 978-1-4339-1970-1 (lib. bdg.)
    ISBN-10: 1-4339-2163-4   ISBN-13: 978-1-4339-2163-6 (soft cover)
    1.Jonas Brothers (Musical group)—Juvenile literature. 2. Rock musicians—
    United States—Biography—Juvenile literature. I. Title.
    ML3930.J62K44   2010
    782.42164092'2—dc22   [B]   2009003210

This edition first published in 2010 by
Gareth Stevens Publishing
A Weekly Reader® Company
1 Reader's Digest Road
Pleasantville, NY 10570-7000 USA

Copyright © 2010 by Gareth Stevens, Inc.

Executive Managing Editor: Lisa M. Herrington
Senior Designer: Keith Plechaty

Photo credits: cover, title page Andrew Marks/Corbis; p. 4 AP Photo/Jennifer Graylock; p. 6 Scott
Lituchy/Star Ledger/Corbis; p. 7 Paul Drinkwater/NBCU Photo Bank via AP Images; p. 8 Kevin Mazur/
WireImage/Getty Images; p. 9 Steven Hockney/Shutterstock; p. 10, 40 Jeff Vespa/WireImage/Getty
Images; p. 12 AP Photo/Peter Kramer; p. 13 Katy Winn/Corbis; p. 14 Jason Merritt/Getty Images; p. 15
AP Photo/Dan Steinberg; p. 16 Frank Mullen/NHLI/Getty Images; p. 18 Kevin Winter/Getty Images;
p. 19 Frank Trapper/Corbis; p. 20 Erik C. Pendzich/Rex USA, courtesy Everett Collection; p. 21 AP Photo/
Robert E. Klein; p. 22, 41 AP Photo/Disney World, Mark Ashman; p. 24 Mathew Imaging/FilmMagic/
Getty Images; p. 25 bottom AP Photo/Matt Sayles; p. 26 Disney Channel/courtesy Everett Collection; p. 27
bottom Andresr/Shutterstock; p. 27 top, 46 Andrew Marks/Corbis; p. 28 Chad Batka/Corbis; p. 30 bottom
Kevin Winter/Getty Images for AMA; p. 30 top RoJo Images/Shutterstock; p. 31 AP Photo/Armando
Franca; p. 32 Michael Loccisano/FilmMagic/Getty Images; p. 33 AP Photo/Mark J. Terrill; p. 34 AP Photo/
Evan Agostini; p. 36 Disney Channel/courtesy Everett Collection; p. 38 Mark Blinch/Reuters/Corbis; p. 39
bottom adfd/Shutterstock; p. 39 top Rena Schild/Shutterstock; p. 44 Yevgeny Gultaev/Shutterstock

All rights reserved. No part of this book may be reproduced, stored in a retrieval system, or
transmitted in any form or by any means, electronic, mechanical, photocopying, recording, or
otherwise, without the prior written permission of the copyright holder. For permission, contact
permissions@gspub.com.

Printed in the United States of America

1 2 3 4 5 6 7 8 9 14 13 12 11 10 09

Contents

Words in the glossary appear in **bold** type the first time they are used in the text.

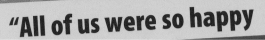

"All of us were so happy **TO HAVE FULFILLED OUR DREAM.**"

—The Jonas Brothers

The Jonas Brothers are among the most recognizable musical groups in the world.

Chapter 1

Big Brothers

For Kevin, Joe, and Nick Jonas, it was a night to remember. On March 22, 2008, a sea of people spread out before them at the Izod Center in North Rutherford, New Jersey. Screaming fans waved cell phones as lights in time to the music. The three brothers stood onstage and belted out the words to "We Are the Champions."

The classic hit by the rock band Queen summed up the brothers' feelings perfectly. It was the last night of their Look Me in the Eyes Tour. The Jonas Brothers were on top of the world! The Izod Center was the closest concert **venue** to their hometown of Wyckoff, New Jersey. Growing up, they would go there to see shows. The brothers often dreamed of playing there themselves one day.

▲ The Jonas Brothers' energetic performances keep their fans coming back for more.

TRUE OR FALSE?

The Jonas Brothers have performed at the White House.

For answers, see page 46.

Making Headlines

When the day finally came for them to play the Izod Center, it was the Jonas Brothers' first tour as a **headlining band**. On other tours, they had opened for bigger acts. This time, the brothers were the stars of the show.

The 20,000-seat arena sold out quickly. It was packed with fans, friends, and family. For the final song, the brothers invited everyone they knew onstage to join them.

Dreams Come True

It was an emotional moment for the brothers. They had finally achieved their dream. They realized just how far they had come. "Everyone was crying because it was the end to such an awesome tour," the brothers write in their book *Burning Up: On Tour With the Jonas Brothers*. "All of us were so happy to have fulfilled our dream of playing that arena. … That night in New Jersey was the end of our tour, but it was also the beginning of something amazing. It was the start of who we're going to be for years to come."

Fact File

In 2008, the Jonas Brothers played during the halftime show for the Thanksgiving Day NFL football game.

Prime-Time Performances

Audiences around the world can't seem to get enough of the brothers. But sold-out concerts aren't the only place to see the Jonas Brothers' energetic live act. They also perform on many popular TV shows. Some of the shows they have appeared on include *Saturday Night Live*, *The Ellen DeGeneres Show*, *The Tonight Show With Jay Leno*, and *Jimmy Kimmel Live*.

▲ The Jonas Brothers appear on *The Tonight Show With Jay Leno* in August 2008.

On the Road to Fame

The Jonas Brothers burst onto the music scene in 2007. Soon they were performing with Miley Cyrus, Taylor Swift, and other talented young artists. Their success didn't come overnight, however. Nick and Joe took to the stage at an early age. Both performed in musical theater. The three brothers played small concerts at schools to get noticed.

Their first big break was a **recording deal** with Columbia. But that turned into heartbreak when their first album didn't take off.

▼ In 2007, the Jonas Brothers toured with Miley Cyrus in the Best of Both Worlds Tour.

Headed for the Top

The Jonas Brothers' second album, *Jonas Brothers*, sold more than 1 million copies in 2007. When an album sells that many copies, the Recording Industry Association of America certifies the album as **platinum**. Talk show host Ellen DeGeneres presented a platinum album award to the Jonas Brothers on her show. The show aired on January 21, 2008. She also gave Joe Jonas a crash helmet with a microphone. Joe is accident prone. He has fallen onstage more than once!

▲ Ellen DeGeneres was almost as excited to have the Jonas Brothers on her show as they were to be there.

A New Beginning

A new recording deal with Disney's Hollywood Records gave them a second chance. The Jonas Brothers toured the world. They set records for selling out big concert arenas. Their singles topped the charts, and their albums sold millions. Fans tuned in to watch them on TV, too.

By the end of 2008, they were filming a new Disney Channel comedy show called *JONAS*. They were also celebrating their first **Grammy Award** nomination, for best new artist. "We wake up every morning excited because we get to do what we love," Kevin has said.

Kevin says his secret goal is to be an astronaut. It's a goal he shares with Lance Bass, former member of the band *NSYNC.

"**Our success is very much** **A GROUP EFFORT.**"

—The Jonas Brothers

Denise Jonas accompanies her sons to the 2009 Grammy Awards.

Chapter 2

Making Music Together

Music has always been an important part of the Jonas family's life. The brothers' parents, Kevin and Denise, met at a Christian college in Dallas, Texas. Denise sang in her church choir. Kevin was a minister and cofounder of a Christian music record label.

Kevin's work took the family all over the country, so the couple's children were born in different cities. Paul Kevin II was born on November 5, 1987, in Teaneck, New Jersey. Joseph Adam (Joe) was born in Casa Grande, Arizona, on August 15, 1989. Nicholas Jerry (Nick) was born on September 16, 1992, in Dallas, Texas. The family returned to New Jersey when Kevin Sr. took a job at a church in Wyckoff.

TRUE OR FALSE?

All the Jonas Brothers were homeschooled by their mother.

Brotherly Love

The brothers consider Wyckoff to be their hometown. As a young teen, Kevin was a bit of a loner. In an interview with *People* magazine, he described himself as being "such a dork." He could always count on his brother Joe to make him laugh, though. Joe is the family comedian. Nick has always been the most driven to succeed. His family nicknamed him "the president" because he seems to be so ambitious.

In 2000, youngest brother Franklin Nathaniel was born. Frankie has a couple of nicknames. He's known as the Bonus Jonas. His family calls him Frank the Tank. Frankie used to call himself Frankie Jonas Rockstar Guy.

◀ Little brother Frankie is lovingly called the Bonus Jonas by his family.

All About Kevin

Name: Paul Kevin Jonas II

Birth date: November 5, 1987

Birthplace: Teaneck, New Jersey

Height: 5 feet 8 inches (173 cm)

Eyes: Hazel

Hair: Brown

Instrument: Lead guitar; also vocals

Hobby: Collecting Gibson Les Paul guitars

Stagestruck

The Jonas family has always enjoyed playing music together and singing. Kevin Sr. and Denise quickly realized that their boys had talent. From an early age, the brothers starred in TV commercials.

Nick, especially, was drawn to performing onstage. He remembers once giving a performance while standing on the coffee table at his grandmother's house. "She was like, 'Get down or you're going to hurt yourself,' " Nick told the *Star-Ledger*. "And I said, 'No, I've got to practice. I'm going to be on Broadway.' " He was only three at the time. By age six, he was putting on shows in the family basement.

Fact File

Kevin was teased a lot as a kid because his ears stuck out. Other kids called him "Spock ears." This referred to the pointy-eared character, Mr. Spock, on the 1960s *Star Trek* TV series.

All About Joe

Name: Joseph Adam Jonas

Birth date: August 15, 1989

Birthplace: Casa Grande, Arizona

Height: 5 feet 10 inches (178 cm)

Eyes: Brown

Hair: Black

Instruments: Tambourine, keyboard, some guitar; also vocals

Hobbies: Filmmaking, making home movies

TRUE OR FALSE?

Kevin used a book called *Teach Yourself Guitar* to teach himself to play the instrument at age 13.

A Star Is Born

Nick's singing attracted attention when he was just six years old. A woman overheard him singing at a barbershop while he was getting a haircut. She suggested his parents get in touch with a talent agent she knew.

Before long, Nick was headed for Broadway. He landed parts in hit musicals, including *Annie Get Your Gun* and *Beauty and the Beast*. By the time he turned 10, Nick had spent three years performing in Broadway shows. His success inspired Joe to try out for musical theater, too. Joe landed a part in a Broadway production of the opera *La Boheme*.

Holiday Cheer

At age 10, Nick wrote and recorded a Christmas song with his dad called "Joy to the World (A Christmas Prayer)." The song was played on Christian radio stations. Soon Columbia Records executives wanted to produce a solo album by Nick for the Christian music market. Then Joe and Kevin got in on the act. The executives decided to offer a recording deal to all three in 2005.

Fact File

In September 2004, Nick performed his song "Dear God" at the United Nations in New York City.

Dad Rocks!

The brothers grew up listening to all kinds of music, including Christian, rock, country, pop, and soul. They say they were influenced by singer-songwriters Elvis Costello, Johnny Cash, and Stevie Wonder. Other influences included Keith Urban, Garth Brooks, John Mayer, Prince, and Paul McCartney. The Jonas Brothers like songs that tell stories. That might be why they've always written their own music. "Our success is very much a group effort. It may come as a surprise that we actually prefer it that way ... like the Three Musketeers, we're all for one and one for all." The brothers say their dad is their **mentor**.

▲ Kevin Sr. (second from left) appreciates all kinds of music. His kids grew up listening to a variety of singers.

"I ... wondered if I could **CONTINUE MAKING MUSIC.**"

—Nick Jonas

Fans in Atlanta, Georgia, cheer for the Jonas Brothers.

Chapter 3
Single-Minded Ambition

Like many up-and-coming bands, the Jonas Brothers thought that signing a record deal would make them stars. But success was not as easy as that. There was still hard work ahead of them.

After being signed, the boys spent most of 2005 on tour. They performed across the country with bands like the Backstreet Boys, Aly & AJ, and the Cheetah Girls. At that point, few people had heard of the Jonas Brothers. They spent most of their time playing schools and small clubs. Sometimes only a handful of people would show up at a club. Other times, the Jonas Brothers would play 8 A.M. concerts at middle schools. They quickly learned how to wake up an audience!

Bad News for the Brothers

Halfway through the 2005 tour, the family noticed a change in Nick. He was moody and irritable. He felt thirsty all the time. He went to the bathroom a lot. He also began losing weight. In less than three weeks, he lost about 15 pounds (7 kilograms).

Tests later revealed that Nick had **type 1 diabetes.** "To suddenly have the shock of diabetes was a bit overwhelming in itself," Nick said. "I also wondered if I could continue making music … but I had the support of my friends and the band to be there with me." His mom stayed with him every night at the hospital.

Fact File

The Jonas Brothers' hit song "A Little Bit Longer" is about finding a cure for diabetes.

▼ Nick was shocked to find out he has type 1 diabetes. He quickly learned how to treat the disease.

All About Nick

Name: Nicholas Jerry Jonas

Birth date: September 16, 1992

Birthplace: Dallas, Texas

Height: 5 feet 6 inches (168 cm)

Eyes: Brown

Hair: Brown

Instruments: Guitar, piano, drums; lead vocals

Hobby: Golf (His dream is to be a professional golfer.)

Turning Lemons Into Lemonade

People with type 1 diabetes don't produce **insulin**. Insulin is a hormone that turns sugar and starches from food into energy the body needs to survive. It is a serious disease, but it can be controlled with proper treatment.

Nick wanted to help other kids with diabetes. So the Jonas Brothers founded Change for the Children and D-Vision. Change for the Children helps kids facing all kinds of challenges. D-Vision is one part of that. It raises awareness about diabetes. "We wanted to let them know that despite major problems like diabetes or cancer, you can succeed," Nick has said.

TRUE OR FALSE?

These days the Jonas Brothers like only sold-out arenas. They never play to small audiences.

▲ The brothers' songs quickly landed on *Billboard* music charts.

Hitting the Top 10

Billboard magazine publishes charts, or lists, of the most popular singles and albums. The Jonas Brothers have made it on the charts more than once. As of 2009, three of their songs have reached the top 10, as have three of their albums. The album *A Little Bit Longer* has even reached number one!

Hits and Losses

On December 27, 2005, the Jonas Brothers released their first single, "Mandy." Columbia Records released the brothers' first album, *It's About Time*, in August 2006. It sold just 62,000 copies.

Columbia executives were unhappy. After just one year, the record label ended its contract with the Jonas Brothers. The band continued to tour, but money was tight. "Our savings were spent, credit cards were maxed out. We were selling T-shirts for gasoline money at every gig," Kevin Sr. recalled.

Fact File

The Jonas Brothers' first single, "Mandy," reached number four on MTV's popular show *Total Request Live.*

Welcome to Disney

The Jonas Brothers rebounded quickly. In February 2007, they signed with Disney's Hollywood Records. Disney has a lot of experience turning young artists into stars. But the Jonas Brothers were different.

So-called **boy bands** are often pulled together by a **producer** to attract teens and preteens. The Jonas Brothers were already an experienced rock band. Unlike many teen pop artists, they also wrote and recorded their own songs. "We're not an 'act,' " the brothers say. "We're just three brothers from New Jersey who are living our dream."

TRUE OR FALSE?

The Jonas Brothers once opened for fellow boy band *NSYNC.

▼ New Kids on the Block made a comeback in 2008.

Let's Hear It for the Boys!

Since the 1990s, the term *boy band* has been used to describe popular young male pop groups. Here are some of the most famous boy bands, followed by the year they hit it big.

The Jackson 5 (1969)

New Edition (1983)

New Kids on the Block (1988)

Boyz II Men (1991)

Backstreet Boys (1997, United States; 1995, Europe)

*NSYNC (1998)

"We had found the perfect home with Hollywood Records

AND THE RIDE WAS JUST BEGINNING."

—The Jonas Brothers

The brothers perform at Disney World in 2007.

Chapter 4

It's a Small World After All

Signing on with Disney proved to be just what the Jonas Brothers needed. Disney's Hollywood Records seemed a natural choice for them. The Jonas Brothers had been popular on Radio Disney since the release of their first album. The video for their song "Year 3000" was already a popular video on the Disney Channel.

Disney helped the Jonas Brothers reach a bigger audience. In 2007, the Jonas Brothers' song "Kids of the Future" was part of the soundtrack for the movie *Meet the Robinsons*. "We had found the perfect home with Hollywood Records and the ride was just beginning," the Jonas Brothers wrote in their book, *Burning Up*.

Fact File

Nick wrote the
hit single "S.O.S."
in less than 15
minutes after a
bad date.

Hitting the Big Time

In August 2007, Hollywood Records released *Jonas Brothers*. Within a week of its release, the new album reached number five on *Billboard*'s Hot 200 chart. The first single, "S.O.S.," quickly became the number-one song downloaded on iTunes. The band soon went on tour as an **opening act** for Miley Cyrus. The brothers played 54 concerts on the Disney star's sold-out Best of Both Worlds Tour.

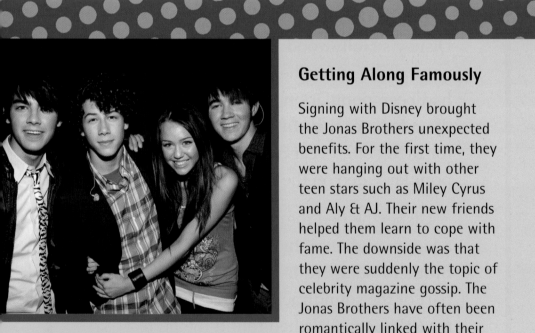

▲ The brothers toured with Miley Cyrus on her Best of Both Worlds Tour.

Getting Along Famously

Signing with Disney brought the Jonas Brothers unexpected benefits. For the first time, they were hanging out with other teen stars such as Miley Cyrus and Aly & AJ. Their new friends helped them learn to cope with fame. The downside was that they were suddenly the topic of celebrity magazine gossip. The Jonas Brothers have often been romantically linked with their touring partners and costars. In a 2008 interview, Miley confessed that she and Nick had dated for two years.

Joe's Favorites

✔ **Ice Cream:**
   Chocolate marshmallow
✔ **Movie:** *Four Feathers*
✔ **Sport:** Soccer
✔ **Performer:** Mick Jagger of the
   Rolling Stones

The Real World

In 2008, the brothers starred in a reality TV series. It was called *Jonas Brothers: Living the Dream*. The first show aired on the Disney Channel on May 16. It gave fans a behind-the-scenes look at the band's life on the road. Cameras followed the family around, capturing concerts, press events, and days off. That same year, the band wrote about their tour in a book called *Burning Up*.

TRUE OR FALSE?

The first CD Joe ever bought was by Hilary Duff.

▶ Fans loved the chance to get a behind-the-scenes look at the brothers in their reality series.

TRUE OR FALSE?

When it first aired, *Camp Rock* was the Disney Channel's most-watched movie that wasn't a sequel.

▼ The Jonas Brothers star in *Camp Rock* with Demi Lovato.

Gone Camping!

In 2008, the Jonas Brothers made their film debut in the Disney Channel movie *Camp Rock*. The made-for-TV movie features teen celebrity Demi Lovato as an aspiring singer. Her character is accepted into a fancy summer camp for musicians. Joe Jonas plays a spoiled rock star who is teaching at the camp as a guest counselor. All three Jonas brothers are in the film. They perform as members of a pop group called Connect 3.

◀ The brothers arrive for a screening of *Camp Rock*.

Video Stars

The movie was a huge hit for Disney. Almost 9 million viewers watched it. Disney launched the Jonas Brothers' video for "Burnin' Up" following the film. *Camp Rock*'s record-setting audience helped launch the video to the number-one spot on iTunes. It has been viewed on YouTube more than 1 million times!

Kevin's Favorites

✔ **Ice Cream:** Rocky Road

✔ **Movie:** *About a Boy*

✔ **Sport:** Golf

✔ **Performer:** John Mayer

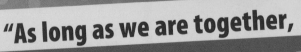

"As long as we are together, **WE ARE HOME, REGARDLESS OF WHERE WE ARE.**"

—The Jonas Brothers

The brothers' busy lives keep them on the road. But the family travels together as much as possible.

Chapter 5

On the Road

The Jonas Brothers spent most of 2007 on the road. In 2008, they set out on their first headlining tour, Look Me in the Eyes. The tour took them from Arizona to New Jersey, and lasted from January 31 to March 22. The boys toured again that summer in the Burning Up Tour. It took them to 43 cities in the United States. Concerts were sold out.

The schedule was hectic. The brothers often had to get up as early as 4 A.M. to do radio or TV interviews. Then they needed to get ready for the concert that night. The stage needed to be set up and the band had to get ready to play. They performed until late at night. Then they tried to catch a few hours of sleep on the tour bus.

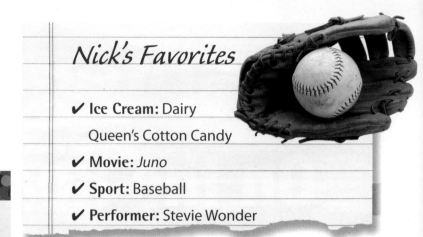

Nick's Favorites

✔ **Ice Cream:** Dairy Queen's Cotton Candy

✔ **Movie:** *Juno*

✔ **Sport:** Baseball

✔ **Performer:** Stevie Wonder

Fact File

Joe is a certified New Jersey babysitter.

A Family Affair

When the brothers go on tour, their family goes with them, including little brother Frankie. Their dad is the band's manager. Their mom is their teacher and a source of moral support. "As long as we are together, we are home, regardless of where we are," the brothers say.

▼ In spite of their stardom, the brothers stay grounded because of their parents' influence.

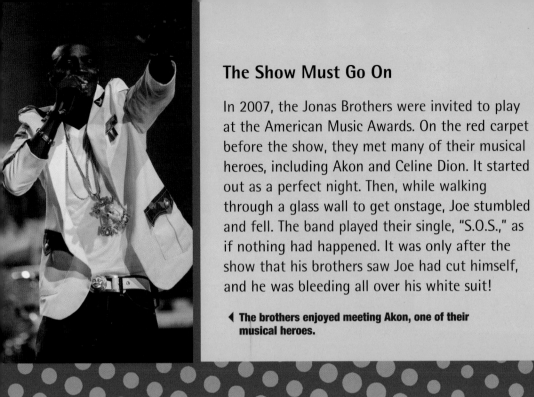

The Show Must Go On

In 2007, the Jonas Brothers were invited to play at the American Music Awards. On the red carpet before the show, they met many of their musical heroes, including Akon and Celine Dion. It started out as a perfect night. Then, while walking through a glass wall to get onstage, Joe stumbled and fell. The band played their single, "S.O.S.," as if nothing had happened. It was only after the show that his brothers saw Joe had cut himself, and he was bleeding all over his white suit!

◀ The brothers enjoyed meeting Akon, one of their musical heroes.

Home on the Highway

On the road, "home" is the tour bus. It's where the family sleeps, eats, and relaxes. Their bus has a built-in recording studio. The brothers can actually record new songs they write while on the road. Most of their 2008 album *A Little Bit Longer* was recorded right on the bus.

TRUE OR FALSE?

The brothers play all of the instruments on their albums.

Before they hit the big time, though, the brothers had to drive themselves to shows. Once, when trying to find someplace to eat after a show, they got lost. "We drove I think two hours away from our hotel by accident," says Joe. "It was pretty funny."

▲ Nick and Joe Jonas talk with fans at MTV Studios in New York City.

A Rock-Star Moment

One of the Jonas Brothers' all-time favorite shows was the 2007 concert at the Texas State Fair. Fans reportedly started arriving at 2 A.M., to try to find spots close to the stage. Despite the heat, the crowd grew to 50,000 by concert time. Traffic was so bad that the brothers had to take a helicopter to get to the concert on time! "As we got closer, we could see thousands of people from the air, but we had no idea just how many there were. The whole scene felt like a true rock-star moment for us," the brothers said.

TRUE OR FALSE?

The Jonas Brothers' 2008 concert in Los Angeles sold out in 20 minutes.

Fan-tastic!

In 2008, the brothers released their third album, *A Little Bit Longer*. It debuted at number one on the *Billboard* charts. In just a week, it sold more than 500,000 copies.

The same year, the Jonas Brothers won six Teen Choice Awards. Fans vote directly for their favorites.

"We love music, touring, and traveling. But most of all, we wake up every day thinking about how much we appreciate the dedication of our fans," the brothers have said.

Fact File

In 2008, the Jonas Brothers won the T-Mobile Breakthrough Artist Award. The winner was decided by fans, who voted by text message.

▲ The Jonas Brothers perform with Stevie Wonder at the 2009 Grammy Awards.

High Honors

In 2008, the brothers were stunned to learn that they had been nominated for a Grammy Award in the best new artist category. Adele, a young singer, won the award. But the brothers were excited to be nominated and thrilled to perform with Stevie Wonder at the 2009 Grammy Awards. "When you start in a band as an artist you say, 'One day, I'll be nominated for a Grammy,' " Nick told MTV News.

"There's always something brand-new COMING AROUND THE CORNER."

—Kevin Jonas

The brothers make an appearance on MTV's *Total Request Live* in 2008.

Chapter 6

What's Next?

Fame has changed the Jonas Brothers' lives in many ways. The family moved to California in 2007, to be close to Disney's filming locations. By the end of 2008, they had toured the world, made two hit albums, and earned about $12 million. They were also on their way to becoming TV and movie stars.

Not bad for three Jersey boys who grew up playing music together in their family's basement. "There's always something brand-new coming around the corner. Who would have guessed we'd be writing a book or starring in movies? It's amazing how fast things can happen in life," Kevin wrote in *Burning Up*.

HUNTINGTON CITY TOWNSHIP
PUBLIC LIBRARY
255 WEST PARK DRIVE
HUNTINGTON, IN 46750

Lights, Camera, Action

In 2009, the Jonas Brothers were focused on film. On February 27, Disney released *Jonas Brothers: The 3D Concert Experience*. The film gave fans a behind-the-scenes look at the Jonas Brothers on tour.

The boys also turned their attention to television. Joe had always dreamed of acting in a comedy. That dream came true when the Jonas Brothers began filming a new show for the Disney Channel. The show, called *JONAS*, first aired on May 2, 2009. The brothers play Kevin, Joe, and Nick Lucas, who live on Jonas Street. The characters are members of a successful teenage band trying to have normal lives. That's not a stretch for the Jonas Brothers!

TRUE OR FALSE?

In 2008, the Jonas Brothers bought a six-bedroom house on a golf course near Dallas, Texas.

▼ The Jonas Brothers appear in an episode of *JONAS*.

36

Movies and Music

June 2009 was a busy month for the Jonas Brothers. Early in the month, the boys starred in *Camp Rock 2*, a follow-up to their first successful Disney movie. This time around, though, the fourth brother got in on the act. Frankie had a part in *Camp Rock 2*. He will also appear with his brothers in *Walter the Farting Dog*. That film is based on a popular children's book.

The Jonas Brothers also released their fourth album, *Lines, Vines, and Trying Times*. The brothers had worked hard on their sound. "We're trying to learn as much as we can, continuing to grow," Nick has said. After the album was released, the brothers set out on a world tour.

▲ The Jonas Brothers perform with guest Taylor Swift in *Jonas Brothers: The 3D Concert Experience.*

As of early 2009, the largest audience the Jonas Brothers had played for was in Mexico City, Mexico. About 80,000 people attended the December 2008 concert.

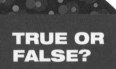
▲ The brothers sign autographs for a crowd of fans in Toronto, Canada.

TRUE OR FALSE?

Joe says if he wasn't a musician, he'd be an airline pilot.

Enjoying the Ride

Kevin Jonas Sr. likes to say, "Even if you're at the top, live like you're at the bottom." His sons take that advice to heart. They know from experience that the music business can be a roller-coaster ride. Plenty of bands have blazed to the top of the charts. Then their fans moved on, and the bands went down in flames. According to Kevin, Nick Carter from the Backstreet Boys offered the best advice. "He said to us, 'Watch the mistakes of the people you admire the most and don't make those same mistakes,' " Kevin explained.

Looking Forward

Joe, especially, is looking forward to the future. "I think the thing that's really going to help us is the fact that we write our own songs and we're in the studio when they're produced, and we're writing songs for other artists right now," he told the *Star-Ledger*. For now, the Jonas Brothers are holding on tight and enjoying the ride. "I realize I'm living every kid's dream," Nick writes in *Burning Up*, "and I am truly grateful for the opportunity."

▲ The Jonas Brothers are looking forward to whatever the future brings.

By the Numbers

62,000 Number of copies their first album sold

80,000 Largest concert audience as of 2009

More than 1 million Number of copies their second album sold

8.9 million Number of viewers for the debut of *Camp Rock*

$12 million Amount of money the Jonas Brothers made in 2007

Time Line

1987 Paul Kevin Jonas II is born November 5 in Teaneck, New Jersey.

1989 Joseph Adam (Joe) Jonas is born August 15 in Casa Grande, Arizona.

1992 Nicholas Jerry (Nick) Jonas is born September 16 in Dallas, Texas.

1999 Nick Jonas makes his first appearance on Broadway in *Annie Get Your Gun*.

2005 The Jonas Brothers sign with Columbia Records.

2006 The Jonas Brothers release their first album.

2007 The Jonas Brothers sign with Disney's Hollywood Records. Their second album is released. The band tours with Miley Cyrus.

2008 The brothers release their third album, tour as headliners, publish a book, and are nominated for a Grammy Award.

2009 Disney releases *Jonas Brothers: The 3D Concert Experience*. The brothers star in *JONAS* and release their fourth album.

Glossary

boy bands: popular young male pop groups. Many of these bands are put together by music producers.

Grammy Award: the highest honor in the music recording business

headlining band: the main act on a concert tour. A headlining band may tour by itself or feature other bands that open the show.

insulin: a hormone that converts sugar and starches into energy the body needs to survive

mentor: someone who teaches, advises, and guides another person

opening act: a band that performs at the start of a show before the headlining band

platinum: refers to an album that has sold 1 million copies

producer: a person who is in charge of making an album, film, or theatrical show

recording deal: an agreement signed between a musical artist and a recording company or record label. The record label produces and promotes the album.

type 1 diabetes: a disease in which the body does not produce enough insulin

venue: the site at which an event is held. A concert venue could be a club, a stadium or arena, a theater, a festival, or a fair.

To Find Out More

Books

Jonas, Joe, Kevin Jonas, and Nick Jonas. *Burning Up: On Tour With the Jonas Brothers*. New York: Disney Hyperion Books, 2008.

Magid, Jennifer. *Miley Cyrus/Hannah Montana*. Pleasantville, NY: Gareth Stevens, 2008.

Web Sites

Change for the Children Foundation
www.changeforthechildren.org
Find out more about how Nick is helping to raise awareness about juvenile diabetes.

The Jonas Brothers
www.jonasbrothers.com
Find news, music, photos, and more on the Jonas Brothers' official site.

MySpace: The Jonas Brothers
www.myspace.com/jonasbrothers
The brothers' MySpace page includes a blog, music, videos, and recorded messages.

DVD
Camp Rock (Disney, 2008)

Publisher's note to educators and parents: Our editors have carefully reviewed these web sites to ensure that they are suitable for children. Many web sites change frequently, however, and we cannot guarantee that a site's future contents will continue to meet our high standards of quality and educational value. Be advised that children should be closely supervised whenever they access the Internet.

Major Awards

American Music Awards

2008 Breakthrough Artist

Kids' Choice Awards

2008 Favorite Music Group

Teen Choice Awards

2008 Choice Breakout Group

2008 Choice Male Red Carpet Icon

2008 Choice Male Hotties

2008 Choice Music Single
("When You Look Me in the Eyes")

2008 Choice Music Love Song
("When You Look Me in the Eyes")

2008 Choice Summer Song ("Burnin' Up")

Source Notes

p. 7 Joe, Kevin, and Nick Jonas, *Burning Up: On Tour With the Jonas Brothers* (New York: Disney Hyperion Books, 2008), 142.

p. 9 Jonas Brothers MySpace blog and recorded messages, www.myspace.com/jonasbrothers.

p. 12 top *People* magazine online, www.people.com/people/jonas_brothers.

p. 12 bottom Nancy Gavilanes, "NJ Boy's Gift Makes Room for Him on National Stage," *Tri-State Voice*, January 2005, http://www.tristatevoice.com/Archives_1_2005.htm#NJ%20Boy's%20Gift%20Makes%20Room%20For%20Him%20on%20National%20Stage.

p. 13 Jay Lustig, "Izod Center is sold out for Jonas Brothers of Wyckoff," *New Jersey Star-Ledger*, March 20, 2008.

p. 15 *Burning Up*, 86.

p. 18 "Jonas Brothers Band Member Reveals He Has Diabetes at Diabetes Research Institute Fundraiser," Children with Diabetes, March 11, 2007, www.childrenwithdiabetes.com/pressreleases.

p. 19 City of Hope, www.cityofhope.org/about/publications/news/Pages/jonas-brothers-change-for-the-children-foundation-donates-250000-dollars-for-diabetes-research-at-city-of-hope.aspx.

p. 20 Sharon Cotliar, "Growing Up Jonas," *People*, June 25, 2008.

p. 21 *Burning Up*, 8.

p. 23 *Burning Up*, 7.

p. 30 *Burning Up*, 130.

p. 31 top Shawn Adler, "Jonas Brothers Celebrate First Grammy Nomination With a 'Big Fist Pump,'" MTV News, December 4, 2008, www.mtv.com/news/articles/1600681/20081204/jonas_brothers.jhtml.

p. 31 bottom Gavilanes, "NJ Boy's Gift."

p. 32 *Burning Up*, 57.

p. 33 *Burning Up*, 8.

p. 35 *Burning Up*, 95.

p. 37 www.billboard.com/bbcom/news/jonas-brothers-fourth-album-due-june-15-1003952570.story

p. 38 top *Burning Up*, 43.

p. 38 bottom Lustig, "Izod Center is sold out."

p. 39 top Lustig, "Izod Center is sold out."

p. 39 bottom *Burning Up*, 45.

True or False Answers

Page 6 True.

Page 12 True.

Page 14 True.

Page 19 False. They often perform "super secret shows" for audiences of about 1,200.

Page 21 False. They opened for the Backstreet Boys.

Page 25 False. Joe's first CD was by Britney Spears.

Page 26 True.

Page 31 False. They have a backup band.

Page 32 False. The concert sold out in just two minutes!

Page 36 True.

Page 38 False. He would be a sailboat captain.

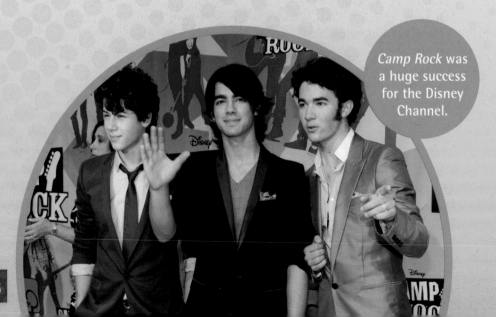

Camp Rock was a huge success for the Disney Channel.

Index

About the Author

Jayne Keedle worked as a music critic and newspaper journalist, then as an editor for *Weekly Reader*. She makes her home in Connecticut with husband, Jim, and stepdaughter, Alma. As a freelance writer and editor, she has written a number of books for young adults.